AF748842

Routledge Revivals

Marriage and Divorce

First published in 1936, *Marriage and Divorce* examines the evolution of marriage and divorce through historical, legal, and cultural lenses. From ancient traditions and Mosaic law to Roman practices, Henry VIII's reforms, and modern judicial processes, the book provides a detailed analysis of how marriage and divorce have advanced over time. Concluding with recommendations for future reforms, this work is an insightful resource for understanding the complexities of marital and legal history.

Marriage and Divorce

The English Point of View

The Rt. Hon. Lord Merrivale

ROUTLEDGE REVIVALS
Routledge
Taylor & Francis Group

First published in 1936
by George Allen & Unwin Ltd.

This edition first published in 2026 by Routledge
4 Park Square, Milton Park, Abingdon, Oxon, OX14 4RN

and by Routledge
605 Third Avenue, New York, NY 10158

Routledge is an imprint of the Taylor & Francis Group, an informa business

© Lord Merrivale, 1936

All rights reserved. No part of this book may be reprinted or reproduced or utilised in any form or by any electronic, mechanical, or other means, now known or hereafter invented, including photocopying and recording, or in any information storage or retrieval system, without permission in writing from the publishers.

Publisher's Note
The publisher has gone to great lengths to ensure the quality of this reprint but points out that some imperfections in the original copies may be apparent.

Disclaimer
The publisher has made every effort to trace copyright holders and welcomes correspondence from those they have been unable to contact.

For Product Safety Concerns and Information please contact our EU representative GPSR@taylorandfrancis.com. Taylor & Francis Verlag GmbH, Kaufingerstraße 24, 80331 München, Germany

A Library of Congress record exists under LCCN: 37007868

ISBN: 978-1-041-35317-1 (hbk)
ISBN: 978-1-003-79714-2 (ebk)
ISBN: 978-1-041-35318-8 (pbk)

Book DOI 10.4324/9781003797142

MARRIAGE AND DIVORCE

The English Point of View

THE RT. HON.
LORD MERRIVALE, P.C.

LONDON
GEORGE ALLEN & UNWIN LTD
MUSEUM STREET

FIRST PUBLISHED IN 1936

All rights reserved

PRINTED IN GREAT BRITAIN BY
UNWIN BROTHERS LTD., WOKING

CONTENTS

MARRIAGE AND DIVORCE

THE ENGLISH POINT OF VIEW

"THE union of one man with one woman for life to the exclusion of all others." So Lord Brougham defined marriage a hundred years ago. There was nothing novel in the idea; what gave the pronouncement its value, apart from the eminence of the speaker, was its concise certainty and the truth it embodied as to the relationship on which our social life is based.

Brougham's statement was elemental. Personal competence to marry; how marriage should be celebrated; and the relative rights of the parties—were matters dealt with by ecclesiastical tribunals, as they had been for centuries. What marriage was had never been in doubt. Divorce by judicial process was non-existent.

Brougham spoke at the onset of a new era in English life. The Reform Act of 1832 was the inevitable prelude of far-reaching changes, and among them, after a long time of disputation, came the Matrimonial Causes Act, 1857, giving power to a new tribunal to decree dissolution of marriage. On rare occasions in the seventeenth and eighteenth centuries, and somewhat more frequently in the nineteenth, marriage had been dissolved by Act of Parliament, but until 1857 there had been no other means. An experienced judge, placed in charge of the new jurisdiction, soon made clear the vigorous strictness with which the powers of the Court would be exercised, bearing in mind the public interests involved. "Marriage," he said on one occasion in a well-known case,[1] "is an institution. It confers status "upon the parties and upon the children to issue from it. Though entered upon by individuals it has a public character. It is the basis upon which the framework of society is built, and as such is subject in all countries to general laws which dictate and control its obligations and incidents, independently of the volition of those who enter upon it."

The ideal embodied in the dictum of Lord Brougham and the principle set forth by Lord Penzance are matters of vital concern to-day. There is clamour of individuals—not of the people at large—for systematic relaxations of the old law. There are loud-voiced dogmatists who proclaim their theories in apparent ignorance of all that marriage involves. An enlightened community, though, cannot consciously permit tampering with the foundations of its well-being. Forty-five millions of population—a figure toward which we seem to be steadily advancing—

[1] Mordaunt *v.* Mordaunt, L.R.P. & M. 109.

would mean English households numbering some nine millions; and it is for these millions of households, with their membership of fathers and mothers and children, that the safeguards of marriage must be upheld. The fact of marriage is their foundation, and it is hard to think that in any large proportion of them divorce can be regarded otherwise than with concern, if not loathing.

Day by day marriage goes on as of old. Numbers fluctuate in a limited degree with the varying conditions of the times, but the institution holds its own. It is true, though, that in the last quarter of a century uncontrollable events have had serious reactions upon family life—even in England—and a markedly increased resort to divorce involves one of the outstanding problems of our national life.

In the light of recorded facts it seems strange now that during the first decade of the century current statistics of divorce caused concern to a well-informcd mind. But they had that effect in the case of a very experienced observer, Lord St. Helier, President for many years of the Divorce Division. In an article which he contributed to the *Encyclopaedia Britannica* in about 1910, he wrote of "an increasing tendency to resort to divorce," which he characterised as "alarming." It is true he was not expressing a view generally held by those who had his means of knowledge: the Royal Commission on Divorce and Matrimonial Causes appointed in 1909 said in its Report, issued in 1912, that the rate of increase was "only rather more than the rate of increase of the population," and went on to observe: "We do not think that the standard of morality is lower to-day than it was fifty or sixty years ago." The Commission was unanimously of opinion, though, that where there were grounds for divorce the poorer classes had not proper means of obtaining it. Changes made since in this respect have reformed the situation; with a sure consequence that there would be a large increase in the number of decrees granted. Before the actual statistics can be taken to show a decline in sexual morality these circumstances must be called to mind.

The census in 1911 showed a population in England and Wales of about thirty-six millions, and decrees of divorce averaged about 860 per annum—one among about 8,400 families. The census of 1931 showed a population of about forty millions, still slowly increasing. In 1933 there were 4,042 decrees, and in 1934, 4,199; representing an average of, say, one decree among 2,000 families. In the intervening years, however, extension of facilities for divorce to petitioners unable to find money for costs on the ordinary scale had become fully effective, and the burden of expense in such proceedings had been reduced by statutory enactments which provided for the hearing of divorce suits in the Courts of Assize.

The problem which is brought into view by developments such as have been indicated is being constantly pressed upon us from various quarters and must have attention from those who care for our national well-being. What is designed in this monograph is to present the relevant facts as distinctly as may be, in their true relation to present conditions and, above all, with proper regard to what is involved in the Institution of Marriage. It is seriously called in question by controversialists as to some of its incidents, and when recently the representatives of the Church of England, after deliberate consideration of the matters debated, made a definite declaration of the Church's absolute adherence to the institution as it is, a remarkable criticism was published by an eminent journalist: "The most active party in the Church," he said, "holds a view of marriage widely at variance with that of the majority of thoughtful men and women of to-day. They would do their utmost to enforce it if a new legal position gave them the opportunity. There would be something highly anomalous in the spectacle of an Established Church giving militant support to standards that were countenanced neither by the law of the land nor by the national conscience."

You cannot meet dogma effectively by mere contradictory assertion. But when we are told authoritatively that the declared principles of the Church of England present "a view of marriage widely at variance with that of the majority of thoughtful men and women," we need to ask what is the qualification by which these "thoughtful" people are identified. And when it is asserted that the Church "gives its support to standards countenanced neither by the law of the land nor by conscience," it seems proper to look far enough into the law to see what the standards are which the Church is upholding, and to give some thoughtful consideration to those whose "conscience" is cited to condemn the Church.

HOW MARRIAGE CAME TO BE

THE place of marriage in human life and how marriage came to be are matters easily lost sight of. Marriage was no evolutionary development or organised outcome of human progress. It is founded on words of Divine authority spoken nineteen centuries ago with a certainty quite unmistakable. The Christian era had hardly begun, but the teaching of Our Lord had, and its eager acceptance by simple-minded hearers had gravely disturbed the minds of men in authority. So "among the multitudes assembled in the borders of Galilee beyond Jordan came the Pharisees tempting Him and saying: Is it lawful for a man to put away his wife for any cause?" Their incentive we can only conjecture. They, of course, were in no doubt as to the Mosaic law; "they asked . . . tempting Him." Promptly the position changed. They were called upon to state the law as they knew it. "What did Moses command you?" "And they said, Moses suffered to write a bill of divorcement and put her away." Then came the words of power: "For the hardness of your hearts Moses wrote you this precept. But from the beginning of creation male and female made He them. For this cause shall a man leave his father and mother and shall cleave to his wife; and they twain shall be one flesh; so then they are no more twain but one flesh. What therefore God hath joined together let not man put asunder."

The new commandment perplexed even the disciples of Jesus as the Gospel narratives show. What must have been its reactions among the Jewish multitudes and among those subject to the civil laws of Rome? Jewish law and practice were unmistakably clear. Roman habits of life were perfectly well known.

THE MOSAIC LAW

THE Mosaic law of marriage had two remarkable characteristics. Adultery of a wife was punishable with death: the marriage tie was dissoluble at the will of the husband.[1] A distinguished writer in our own times, Dr. Edersheim, presents the matter in very striking terms.[2] As to marriage, he says: "The pious fasted before it, confessing their sins." As to divorce, he writes: "The Jewish law unquestionably allowed divorce on almost any ground, the difference being not as to what was lawful, but on what grounds should a man set the law in motion and make use of the absolute liberty which it accorded him . . . The practice was discouraged by many of the Rabbis, alike by their teaching and example; and the ancient Jewish law took watchful care of the interests of the women. . . . A false charge of unchastity would be visited upon the accusing husband by chastisement and amercement; but if the charge was true she was to be stoned to death." Another eminent student, Doctor Edward Westermarck, writes thus:[3] "The right of the hus-

[1] Leviticus xx.10; Deuteronomy xxii. 13–19.

[2] *Life and Times of Jesus*, chap. iv.

[3] *History of Human Marriage*, p. 307.

band to divorce his wife at pleasure was the central thought in the entire system of Jewish divorce law."

Somehow, though the law then was as here stated, there was keen popular interest in the problem about which the Pharisees presented their challenging inquiry. They returned to it at a very late period in the earthly life of Jesus. Bringing to Him "a woman taken in adultery," "when they had set her in the midst they say unto Him: Master, this woman was taken in adultery, in the very act; now Moses commanded us that such should be stoned; but what sayest Thou?" The discomfiture which awaited them need not be dwelt upon.

ROMAN DEGENERACY

AMONG the Romans at the time when our Lord's pronouncement was made, marriage was a merely consensual relationship. In the earliest times, as the Twelve Tables show, the wife was *in manu* of the husband. That involved, as ancient writers say, power on his part of life and death.[1] At any rate, *patria potestas* included absolute power of divorce. Gibbon tells us that the Romans abstained from exercise of this privilege for upwards of five centuries; in fact, until 234 B.C. At length, though, with unprecedented power and prosperity, there came moral degeneracy. Dean Farrar, in his work on the *Early Days of Christianity*,[2] contrasts the earlier and the later conditions. "Family life," he says, "had once been a sacred thing and for five hundred and twenty years divorce had been unknown; but under the Empire marriage had come to be regarded with disfavour and disdain. 'Women,' as Seneca says, 'married in order to be divorced and were divorced in order to marry, and noble Roman matrons counted the years not by the consuls but by discarded or discarding husbands.' "

[1] Livy xxxix. 18; Tacitus xiii. 32; Poste's *Gaius*, title *de manu*.

[2] Cap. 1.

To quote again from Gibbon: "A new jurisprudence was introduced; marriage like other partnerships might be dissolved by abdication of one of the associates." Summing up the course of events, he says: "In three centuries of prosperity and corruption this . . . was enlarged to frequent practice and pernicious abuse. Passion, interest, or caprice, suggested daily motives for the dissolution of marriage; a word, a sign, a message, a letter, the mandate of a freedman, declared the separation; the most tender of human connexions was degraded to a transient society of profit or pleasure. According to the various conditions of life both sexes alternatively felt the disgrace and injury . . . A specious theory is confuted by this free and perfect experiment, which demonstrates that the liberty of divorce does not contribute to happiness and virtue." How striking a declaration from an author so unbiassed. The moral and social laxities of which he wrote not only sapped the strength of a great race; they undermined the power of a mighty Empire.

HOW MARRIAGE PREVAILED

WITHIN the Roman world, and during the unpropitious centuries described by Gibbon, marriage, as Jesus had commanded it, became an institution and an energising power. Under steadfast pagan proscription the Christian family rose into being. As persecution developed into policy, the mode of life of Christians must have been a sure means of their identification. A passage in which Tacitus[1] describes Nero's action when Rome had been burned shows what it meant then to be a Christian: "He laid the fault upon a set of people who were holden in horror for their offences and called by the vulgar 'Christians.' . . . Some who confessed their sect were at first seized, and afterwards vast multitudes, who were convicted not so much of burning Rome as of hatred to mankind." Until Hadrian's reign—A.D. 116–138—Christianity was a crime. For two centuries more the Christian was at the mercy of those in power.

How Christianity prevailed as the centuries rolled on is a matter of historic record. Under the Emperor Constantine—A.D. 324–338—it became the declared religion of the reconsti-

[1] *Vide* Paley's translation.

tuted Empire. Gibbon describes how "the Christian princes adapted their penal statutes to the degrees of moral and religious turpitude. . . . Adultery was declared a capital offence." The real triumph, though, was not that demonstrated in statecraft; it was the establishment if the ordered household on the footing of Christian marriage, and this certainly preceded the changed laws of the later times. When Roman power had vanished, the Christian principle which ruled the homes had come to be accepted as a basic rule of life, not as matter of law. Here in England it was as late as A.D. 946 that the Saxon King Edmund ordained the celebration of marriage with religious rites, and in A.D. 1200 that a Synod of Westminster prescribed the publication of banns. What demonstrates most clearly, perhaps, the merely ancillary nature of the action of States in the establishment of the institution of marriage is this fact, that during long ages the Church held marriage to result from the consent and cohabitation of competent parties. Doctor Darwell Stone, in his work entitled *Christian Dogma*, states the fact thus: "According to the ordinary teaching of the Christian Church," what was "essential . . . to a valid marriage" was "the formal consent of parties free to contract marriage with one another, and this independent of any religious ceremony. . . . The consent must be not a promise only, but consent taking effect at once."

Whether the powerful control exerted by the ecclesiastical authorities and the strict regulations they imposed might have been sufficient if they had retained their ancient power to protect the community against overwhelming laxity in respect of marriage, can only be guessed. What difference the Protestant Reformation made is also largely matter of conjecture. An outstanding fact about which there is no doubt is that laxity became in more modern times a serious danger. Clandestine marriages among the well-to-do developed into a serious menace. That was why in 1753 the Lord Chancellor, Lord Hardwick, framed the well-known Statute, 25 Geo. II, c. 33, which, as far as England is concerned, placed marriage on its modern footing. This Act bears its own testimony to the mischief which had arisen. Among its provisions are these: to solemnise marriage without due publication of banns or episcopal licence was made a felony punishable with transportation, and such a marriage was to be deemed null and void, and no suit might be entertained in an ecclesiastical court to compel celebration *in facie ecclesiae* by reason of any contract of marriage whatsoever, whether *per verba de praesenti* or *per verba de futuro*. To inscribe in a church register a false entry with regard to such a transaction was made punishable with death.

Nearly a century after the passing of Lord Hardwick's Act—which was limited in its operation to England—a litigation arose in the Courts in Ireland in which the question was whether in that country a contract *per verba de praesenti* between competent parties, followed by cohabitation, effected marriage.[1] The case came on appeal to the House of Lords. The judges in the Irish Courts had disagreed; the Lords did the like. The main issue was not whether such action had some effect, but whether to be "valid to all intents" marriage must—apart from Lord Hardwick's Act—be solemnised by a clergyman. Lord Lyndhurst took the view that it must, but said this:

> The first and material point is as to the effect by the law of England previous to the Marriage Act of a marriage *per verba de praesenti*, by which I understand a contract of present marriage, for that is the sense in which these words are used in all the text writers and reports of decisions upon the subject. "*Spousals de praesenti*," Swinburn says, "are a mutual contract or promise of present matrimony; as when the man doth say to the woman, I do take thee to my wife, and she then answereth, I do take thee to my husband.

[1] *Vide* Reg. *v.* Willis, 10 Cl. and Fin. 534.

Such a contract entered into between a man and a woman was indissoluble; the parties could not, by mutual consent, release each other from the obligation. Either party might, by a suit in the spiritual court, compel the other to solemnise *in facie ecclesiae.* It was so much a marriage that if they cohabited together they could not be proceeded against for fornication, but merely for a contempt. If either of them cohabited with another person, the parties might be proceeded against for adultery. The contract was considered to be of the essence of matrimony, and was therefore and by reason of its indissoluble nature styled in the ecclesiastical law *verum matrimonium*, and sometimes *ipsum matrimonium*. Another and most important effect of such a contract was that if either of the parties afterwards married with another person, solemnising the same *in facie ecclesiae*, such marriage might be set aside even after cohabitation and the birth of children and the parties compelled to solemnise the first marriage *in facie ecclesiae*." Such were the effects of a marriage *per verba de praesenti*.

Lord Lyndhurst's pronouncement leaves no doubt as to the old law, and it is interesting to observe that in recent times so eminent an authority on ecclesiastical law as the late Lord Phillimore set forth as his own view, in an article on Canon Law, which he contributed to the *Encyclopaedia Britannica*, the conclusion that before the Marriage Act "the declared consent of the parties to take each other then and there" as husband and wife "contracted although irregularly holy matrimony."

A certain degree of isolation consequent upon legislative repudiation of what was denounced as "the usurped authority of the Bishops of Rome" must be borne in mind when the development—in the juristic sense—of our English laws as to marriage is under consideration. Having been at one with Rome when that event occurred, our people stood fast by the ancient principle independently of Rome. So when the Council of Trent laid down new rules, they had no effect here, though they operated wherever the mandates of Rome were operative.

HENRY VIII AND AFTER

WHEN ancient doctrines came to be distinctly challenged on the uprising of Protestantism among our people, the law as to marriage was not least among the incidents of conflict. Controversies began in Tudor times; went on through the generations of what may be called the Puritan ascendancy, and, indeed, survived in some respects till after the Revolution of 1688. All the time the mind of the English people showed an unwavering firmness as to the institution of marriage. Before King Henry's renunciation of Roman authority the principle had been definitely assailed. One of Wiclif's profounder differences with his spiritual superiors arose in respect of it. Not only was divorce "lawful" in case of adultery, he declared; "it must be held lawful for Christians for many other causes equal to adultery." Notoriously, this view was held by men overseas of the eminence of Luther, Erasmus, and Melanchthon. Its influence was exemplified by happenings in England which ensued upon the legislative enactment under Henry VIII that henceforward England should be governed by "such laws ecclesiastical as shall be thought fit by His Majesty, His Council, and those, or the more part of them, convenient to be used and practised and set forth within this Realm." What were the "laws ecclesiastical" which the King and his agents had in view was not made known by His Majesty's authority during his reign. What was promptly done was to set up by the Statute 25 Hy. VIII, c. 19, the Royal Commission with Archbishop Cranmer at its head—"pro Reformatio Legum Ecclesiasticarum"—with power to abrogate and amend the canon law as the King and the majority of the Commissioners might think fit.

Archbishop Cranmer was not dilatory about his task. Within two years the Commissioners had presented a Report recommending changes of far-extended scope. But the activity had a surprising sequel. King Henry took no action under the Statute. When Edward VI was king, the lapsed powers were renewed by an Act passed in 1550. Again Cranmer exerted himself, but no Royal mandate was signed. Queen Mary's accession rendered Reformatio Legum Ecclesiasticarum in the Cranmerian sense unthinkable. Elizabeth succeeded Mary, and she had reigned for nearly a quarter of a century when, in 1571, the Report of the Royal Commission of 1534 was published. It was published, and so far as the marriage law was concerned, was never acted upon.

The Report *pro Reformatio* covered a wide field. Incidentally, it embodied what we call the Thirty-nine Articles. Its proposals, so far as they are material here, were embodied under the title "De Adulteriis et Divortis." A comprehensive summary of their effect can be found in evidence given by Sir Lewis Dibdin before the Royal Commission of 1909. Formidable penalties for adultery were prescribed—including forfeiture of goods, banishment, and imprisonment for life. Dire penalties for malicious desertion, "deadly hostility," and certain grave offences of immorality, were set forth. Upon the conviction of a spouse for adultery, the innocent party after an interval of six months, or a year, to give opportunity for reconciliation, might remarry. Desertion or prolonged absence of a spouse "without tidings" were recommended as grounds on which there might be leave to remarry, but with the qualification that upon the reappearance of the absentee with satisfactory explanations of his disappearance, the deserted spouse must return. What under the now existing law is called "cruelty" was also to be ground for divorce.

The most effective evidence of the English view as to proposals such as these which were set up in the Report "pro Reformatio," is that nearly three centuries elapsed before any one of the proposed changes was made. Sir Lewis

Dibdin in his evidence before the Royal Commission of 1909 suggested as the probable explanation of it that the recommendations in question in fact had their origin among "foreign Protestants." He said as to this part of the Report: "the conclusion seems to be inevitable that the Reformatio Legum as we have it, so far as the section on Divorce is concerned, is merely a literary relic representing the views derived from continental sources of certain individual churchmen of great eminence and influence." Whether this is or is not the explanation, the recommendations of Cranmer and his colleagues did not command the assent of their fellow-countrymen.

There are incidents in the troubled times which included the later years of Charles I, and the era of the "Commonwealth," which show why contemporary lawgivers adopted the ancient maxim of passivity—"Let well alone." When a Royal Commission recommended that marriage should be solemnised before justices, the idea was said at the time to have been "rejected with scorn." When Puritan spokesmen advocated restoration of the Mosaic Law whereby adultery was punishable with death, nothing came of it.

A remarkable phase in the life of the poet Milton may perhaps be regarded as illustrative of the general opinion in England concerning marriage in the troubled times he witnessed. Milton had married at the age of thirty-five, when the prosperous season which gave the world his earlier poems had passed. In the time of the Commonwealth, when his personal and official influence was of the greatest, finding himself separated from his wife by temperamental differences, he planned a new marriage and made no secret of his design. Forthwith he was warned that such a thing could not be. Thereupon he published his treatise on *The Doctrine and Discipline of Divorce*, setting forth his view that divorce and remarriage were elemental personal rights of the citizen. The keynote is found in the opening chapter, where the author lays down that "indisposition, unfitness, or contrariety of mind, arising from a cause in nature unchangeable, hindering, and ever likely to hinder the main benefits of conjugal society, which are solace and peace, is a greater reason of divorce than natural frigidity, especially if there be no children and that there be mutual consent." Milton's treatise had a remarkable reception. It was formally condemned in Parliament, and the author was warned that he had exposed himself to serious penalties. Thereupon he produced *Tetrachordon*, a review of the vacillations of old times, such as the edicts of the Emperors, now prohibiting divorce and later on warranting divorce by consent. The accepted principle that divorce—*a mensâ et thoro*—might be decreed only for adultery, he attributed to Papal tyranny. "The papal and unjust restriction of divorce," he writes, "need not be dear to us, since the plausible restraining of that was in a manner the first loosing of Antichrist. . . . Nor do we less remarkably owe the first means of his fall here to the contemning of that restraint by Henry the Eighth whose divorce he opposed." Protestants and Papists alike come under the great man's unsparing censure; he finds them involved in the common guilt of "designing to pluck the power and arbitrament from the master of the family into whose hands God and the Law of all Nations put it and . . . authorising a judicial court to toss about and divulge the unaccountable and secret reason of disaffection between man and wife."[1]

The poet in his censures upon the Papacy took no account of the facility with which a decree of nullity—some of the causes for which he indicates—was said to be made in some ecclesiastical tribunals overseas an easy alternative to dissolution of marriage for reasons such as he advised. The English law was against him, as he knew, and so was the English mind.

[1] *Tetrachordon*, Cap. xxi.

HOW CIVIL DIVORCE BEGAN

DURING the centuries between King Henry VIII's renunciation of Papal supremacy and the time when divorce by legal process became part of our judicial procedure, there occurred a series of events—unassociated at the time, no doubt—which can be seen now to have been forecasts of change.

While Henry was still sovereign a curious private Act of Parliament was passed which gave effect in advance to some findings of the Commission "Legum Ecclesiasticarum." The Marquess of Northampton was an outstanding figure at Court; he had obtained in an ecclesiastical court a decree of divorce *a mensâ et thoro* on the ground of his wife's adultery; he desired to remarry; and he petitioned the King that a Commission should be set up to determine whether he "might lawfully remarry." Cranmer was chief of the Commission, and they in accordance with the findings of the earlier Commission, reported in the affirmative. Northampton did as was said he might, and by an Act subsequently passed it was "declared" that the Marquess was at liberty by the laws of God and man to remarry, and "enacted" that the second marriage which he had contracted should "be deemed lawful . . . the said former marriage notwithstanding." The course of events during many generations indicates that the Northampton statute was regarded as a favour to an eminent courtier in an unsettled age rather than as a declaration of the law: long after its occurrence the Northampton case had fateful consequences. When about a century and a half had elapsed, it was invoked in the reign of Charles II as a precedent for parliamentary action to effect divorce. Lord de Roos followed Northampton's example in 1669; in 1692 the Duke of Norfolk in like manner obtained statutory dissolution of his marriage. Isolated instances became more frequent. In the middle years of the eighteenth century they averaged one per annum, and between 1800 and 1850 ninety Divorce Bills became Acts of Parliament. In the meantime, national life had changed. Parliamentary reform and reform in local government had produced an awakened people, and as years passed, one of the anomalies which came to be effectively criticised was that which enabled the wealthy to claim divorce if they had cause, while marriage was for the poor indissoluble.

Public opinion reacted to the facts which have just been outlined during a good many years while reform was in hand. A striking instance is found in the passage where in his *Constitutional History* Hallam deals with the proposals of the Commission pro Reformatio Legum Ecclesiasticarum. "Their scheme of a very important branch of social law," he wrote, "seems far better than our own. Nothing can be more absurd than our modern privilegia, our Acts of Parliament to break the bond between an adulteress and her husband. Nor do I see how you can deny redress to every woman in every case of adultery and desertion." What Hallam advocated took thirty years to come into effect.

There was keen discussion, but not general agreement, and it used to be thought that some scathing comments of an eminent judge—Mr. Justice Maule—helped powerfully to promote the object in view. A man of the poorer classes was charged before him with bigamy. The proofs were unmistakable. The wife of the accused had gone off with another man, leaving him in wretched circumstances, and he had found another mate and contracted a bigamous marriage. The words of the learned judge are on record.[1] "It did appear," he said, "that the prisoner had been hardly used. It was hard for him . . . not to be able to have another wife to live with him, when the former

[1] R. *v.* Hall, *The Times*, April 3, 1843.

had gone off to live in an improper state with another man. But the law was the same for him as it was for a rich man, and was equally open for him through its aid to obtain relief. But as the rich man would have done he also should have pursued the proper means pointed out by law, whereby to obtain redress of his grievances. He should have brought an action against the man who was living in the way stated with his wife, and he should have obtained damages, and then should have gone to the Ecclesiastical Court, and obtained a divorce (which would have done what seemed to have been done already), and then he should have gone to the House of Lords, and proving all his case and the preliminary proceedings have obtained a full and complete divorce, after which he might if he liked have married again. The prisoner might perhaps object to this that he had not the money to pay the expenses, which would amount to about five hundred or six hundred pounds—but this did not exempt him from paying the penalty for committing a felony of which he had been convicted." As the man had brought about the bigamous marriage by representing himself to be a bachelor, he was sent to prison.

As has been said, general English opinion was not easily reconciled to the introduction of a system of judicial divorce. Before the Act of 1857 parliamentary conflict about the matter had been long and bitter, and debate frequent. A Royal Commission appointed in 1850 had recommended legislation and a Bill was introduced, but although Sir Robert Peel's Government supported the measure, it did not pass. Parties were divided not upon political lines but by the personal convictions of their members. As to the Bill of 1857, Lord Lyndhurst would have extended its scope, and Mr. Gladstone, though he had been a member of the Government which originally presented it, was its powerful antagonist. "It is opposed," he said, "to the law of the Church, to the law of nature, and to the law of God." Long afterwards Gladstone, in his *Gleanings of Past Years*, republished an article emphasising this opinion which in 1857 he had contributed to the *Quarterly Review*.

In the House of Lords, Lord Cranworth, the Lord Chancellor, recommended the passage of the Bill, but did so in a speech like the following: "I think recognition of the sanctity of marriage underlies the essentials of our quality as a people. No measure could be more injurious or more calculated to interfere with the social welfare of the country than one which tended to shake the solidity of marriage and the strength of the marriage tie." And Lord Cranworth also quoted some words of Lord Stowell to this effect: "The knowledge that persons united in marriage must continue husband and wife often made them good husbands and wives; necessity was a powerful master in teaching the duties it imposed."

Those who are familiar with the Act of 1857 know that it demonstrates a sincere desire that the new departure should, if possible, conduce to the well-being of the community. There are, for instance, provisions in it which show a steadfast determination to confer benefits on spouses who have really suffered wrong. It was not merely an Act to legalise divorce by judicial decree. It took account of powers the ecclesiastical Courts had long had for the protection of ill-used wives, and it established new rights analogous in a way to some which in ancient times had existed under branches of the Common Law—when "dower," "tierce," "jus relictae," and the "courtesy of England," were more than figments of old privileges. The Act definitely provided for the wife's security in the home, and her title to maintenance, and secured her some rights in respect of the guardianship of children. In the years since 1857 these beneficial provisions have not been weakened: in some respect they have been enlarged.

Mr. Gladstone, in the article concerning marriage and divorce which he wrote in 1857, and to which reference has already been made, wrote of the "prohibition of divorce" as "making the conjugal union not a mere indulgence of taste and provision for enjoyment, but a powerful instrument of discipline and self-subjugation, worthy to take rank in that subtle and wonderful system of appointed means by which the life of man on earth becomes his school for heaven." When the Act of 1857 became law, divorce was no longer prohibited. It did not become popular. Those who realise now the dangers the great statesmen saw to be involved, ponder with growing anxiety on the developments of which they know, and the risks they apprehend, and they are fully aware that the true safeguard of the State to-day against such risks is a sound popular view as to marriage and also as to divorce. If light-hearted indifference should prevail it might wreck the most precious part of our national heritage.

It can justly be said that our English legislation has had regard to the outstanding fact that any means of dissolution of marriage affects the common well-being. That was why, very soon after the Act of 1857, duties were assigned to the King's Proctor, and that officer goes on year by year taking whatever action can be taken to prevent resort to the discreditable devices by which divorce may be brought about in disregard of legal restrictions. Although the performance of these duties does not provoke a great degree of discussion, people of experience know that they are steadfastly discharged with the undoubted effect of preventing abuse of the law which would otherwise be inevitable. Every "intervention" of the King's Proctor is determined upon by one of the judges, and the necessity that this should be done, under a code like our own, is one of the manifest reasons which have led to the maintenance of the separate jurisdiction under which the law of divorce is administered.

HOW DIVORCE HAS ADVANCED

THERE was no headlong rush for divorce when the Act of 1857 became law. Indeed, you may say with fair accuracy that the past quarter of a century witnessed the first sensational developments, and that social happenings in such an epoch do not throw the same light on national character and temperament which normal events supply. From 1857 to 1861 the average number of decrees in a year was about three hundred. That in 1931 decrees should have numbered 3,764—twelve times as many—seems at first sight a portentous thing, seeing that the population had only doubled. But when some of the outstanding changes of the intervening times are brought to mind, it is not so surprising.

The average of decrees in the "early sixties" with a population of about twenty millions—if families are taken at the normal proportion of one-fifth—meant one decree among 13,500 families. In 1881, with a population of about twenty-six millions, the yearly average of decrees was about 590, or one among 8,810 families. In 1891 the population reached twenty-nine millions: the average of decrees was about 760, or one among about 7,630 families. In 1901—population about thirty-two and a half millions—average of decrees under 800: one among about 8,100 families. In 1911—population about thirty-six millions—average of decrees about 860: one among about 8,400 families. It was in the next decade that great changes came.

When recent divorce statistics are cited, some relevant facts—too serious to be forgotten—are apt to be overlooked. The Great War broke up, at its later stages certainly, the home life of England. After the War reforms of judicial procedure were effected which enabled "Poor Persons"—heretofore barred by poverty from incurring substantial liabilities for costs in legal proceedings—to obtain redress for conjugal wrongs at no great expense. Insistent debate about the plight of Poor Persons had been one of the causes which led to the appointment of the Royal Commission of 1909. Lord Gorell, the Chairman, had long been President of the Division of the High Court concerned with Divorce Law, and in the course of evidence he gave he said that the matters most impressed upon him in the long period of his judicial service—it began in 1892—had been hardships arising from procedure, and the disabilities of the poor.

The labours of the Royal Commission, capably as its duties were discharged, resulted in amendments of procedure and removal of some disabilities, but did not produce the results some keen advocates of inquiry had desired. They demonstrated the difficulty of reconciling facile divorce with due maintenance of the integrity of marriage. Few of the witnesses threw any doubt on the importance of the marriage tie. Where many of them differed to a wonderful degree was as to what might be done to make divorce available when marriage had "broken down."

The witnesses before the Royal Commission included people of exceptional personal experience and competence, as, for example, judges, practising lawyers, social workers, magistrates, justices' clerks; and they differed as few people would have thought likely. The clerk of the Liverpool justices was convinced that "extension" of facilities for divorce "would involve danger to the community greater than the advantage it would bring." The gentleman who held the like office in Manchester thought there should be "limited extension." Police-court missionaries from the Metropolitan area who were called were all against extension; one whose work lay in the Westminster area declared that he did not know of a single instance among the cases of domestic infelicity with which he had been concerned where a person of the poorer classes had expressed a desire for enlarged grounds of divorce—or for divorce. The High Court judges who had charge of the jurisdiction over matrimonial causes both gave evidence. The President, Sir John Bigham—afterwards Lord Mersey—approved of enlarged grounds of divorce, but in answer to a question from the present Primate—then Archbishop of York—he said: "The advantages of divorce to the rich are so questionable that I do not care to extend it too much to the poor." He suggested that as to the guilty party in a suit there might be power in the Court to prohibit remarriage. His colleague, Mr. Justice Bargrave Deane, speaking after thirty years of experience of the subject, at the Bar and on the Bench, said this: "I think it is a misfortune the divorce laws were ever passed. The existence of divorce makes people think less of the marriage tie. [They] take the risk . . . because they think they can get rid of it afterwards."

Three people very well known at the time who gave remarkable evidence were Miss Millicent Fawcett, distinguished as a social worker; Mr. Chichele Plowden, a Metropolitan Police Magistrate, and Mr. Maurice Hewlett, the author. Miss Fawcett's opinion was that wherever it is found that the marriage tie has "come practically to an end" divorce should be pronounced at the instance of the parties. Mr. Plowden said this: "Without divorce I look upon marriage as a dangerous, mad gamble. . . . I should be in favour of granting divorce for any clear breach of the marriage contract . . . and by mutual consent where the marriage has failed." Mr. Maurice Hewlett's opinion was not so definitely expressed, but was in effect that the Court should be competent in its discretion to decree divorce as between parties who agreed thereto "provided it was a *bona fide* case." The now Bishop of Durham, Dr. Hensley Henson, gave evidence which in its general tenor agreed with the main recommendations ultimately made in the Majority Report of the Commission.

THE COMMISSION: LORD GORELL

THE most potent force in the Commission was naturally the mind of the Chairman, Lord Gorell. You find in his evidence a model of frankness, as to the course of development his opinions had undergone and as to his conclusions. In the main he based himself on two propositions which Dr. Hensley Henson had advanced: "Whatever can be shown to render impossible the primary objects of marriage is prima facie a sufficient ground for divorce: if so, it follows that the conditions of divorce are properly to be determined by the State in the light of Christian principle with reference to the actual necessities and circumstances of men." The resultant process of argument in Lord Gorell's mind is set forth by him as follows:

> There is no reason why the State should not accept the well-expressed sentence of Modestinus, one of the five great *juris consulti* of the Roman Empire, as a definition of marriage: "Nuptiae sunt conjunctio maris et feminae et consortium omnis vitae divini et humani juris communicatiae."
>
> What is the best method of attaining this ideal? Is it by declaring the marriage tie indissoluble in every case, notwithstanding that events have supervened

upon the marriage which have in fact ended the joint life. . . . Or is it better to recognise the deficiencies of human nature and their consequences and in the interest of the parties, their children, and the State, to permit the dissolution of a legal tie when the whole objects of its formation have been frustrated?

The result of my lengthy examination of the principle so far as it is affected by considerations peculiar to Christians is that . . . the English people of the present day . . . may follow the course taken by all other non Roman Catholic countries in the world, they may regard this most important and most difficult question as a matter of civil polity to be settled under the control of the great principles laid down by Christ on grounds of expediency in relation to the present circumstances of the people, and with due regard for the conscientious difficulties of the minority.

I am thus brought to the point that . . . marriage is dissoluble on some grounds in addition to adultery.

The extended grounds of divorce which Lord Gorell proposed were in substance those recommended in the Majority Report—namely, proof of any of the following causes of complaint:

Adultery.

Wilful desertion for three years.

Cruelty on the part of one of the spouses—meaning thereby such conduct as makes it unsafe for the other to live with the former, and is dangerous to life, limb, or health.

Insanity certified to be incurable, the insane spouse having been continuously confined under the Lunacy Acts for not less than five years; relief on such ground to be limited to men not over sixty years of age and women not over fifty.

Habitual drunkenness of an aggravated form; to be ground for separation and if continuous during three years for divorce (on the footing of incurable insanity).

A death sentence commuted to penal servitude for life.

Enlarged grounds for declaration of nullity of marriage were also presented in the Majority Report, to the effect following:

A. Grounds existent at the time of the celebration of marriage:

(*a*) unsoundness of mind;
(*b*) epilepsy;
(*c*) recurring insanity;
(*d*) venereal disease;
(e) pregnancy of the woman at the time of marriage by a man other than the husband—the latter being ignorant of the fact.

B. Grounds subsequent to the celebration:

(*a*) wilful refusal of consummation;
(*b*) presumption of death.

THE MINORITY REPORT

Almost inevitably, the eminent churchmen who were members of the Commission did not agree with some of the proposals in the Majority Report. A Minority Report was signed by the now Primate, and by two eminent jurists, Sir William Anson and Sir Lewis Dibdin, and any informed reader will be reminded by its contents that opinion in the religious world about divorce does not easily change. Two remarkable pronouncements stand forth:

> The real question at issue is the alternative between the narrow expediency of trying to make the lot of certain parties concerned easier and happier, and the wider expediency of strengthening the family life against influences which are threatening it. There can be no question that hitherto the strength of English social life has been the family—the home. The evidence is reassuring that among the great bulk of the people, especially among the middle class and artisans, the obligations of home life are respected, and home life is pure and consistent.

Facts emphasised in the Minority Report include these: Experience—for example, in the United States—shows that easy divorce does not increase "social purity and happiness," but the contrary; in support of the suggested changes "less than two hundred specific cases within the proposed enlargement had been brought to the notice of the Commission by correspondence during the sittings of the Commission . . ." and "some of these manifestly insupportable."

The broad conclusion in the Minority Report is stated thus: "Apart from such changes as may bring within the reach of all the remedies which the law provides for all there is no effective demand that divorce should be made easier." Only two substantial changes were envisaged: desertion for seven years or upwards under circumstances which warrant an order that death be presumed might be a ground for dissolution of marriage: discovery by one party after the ceremony of marriage that the other was previously insane might be a ground for a declaration of nullity.

Amended procedure in cases of nullity, and some enlargement of the grounds on which it may be declared, as they are dealt with in both Reports of the Commission, form a subject-matter of possible reform which must no doubt engage the attention of all who have under consideration possible changes in the existing law of marriage. To declare a ceremony ineffective has been recognised always as a totally different thing from breaking the bond of marriage. To treat it as an expedient of divorce—as was said to be done overseas during the ages when divorce as such was unknown there—is no doubt a degradation rather than an exaltation of the marital relationship. But the contractual aspect of it ought to be strictly regarded because of the gravity of the issues involved, and must be absolutely open to examination when justice requires that inquiry should be made. Lack of capacity, fraud, and absence of consent, cannot be treated lightly, because a lifelong tie is in question. The principles to be applied are well understood, and it may well be doubted whether there is any logical ground for refusing a declaration of nullity in most if not all the cases specified in the majority Report of the Commission. Strict rules as to entering upon marriage do not tend in any way to lessen its sanctity.

TIME PASSES

MORE than a quarter of a century has passed since the Commission of 1909 took up its task; nearly a quarter of a century since the reports were published. Then came the World War with its searching effects on social order; a new generation has sprung up; and it cannot be said yet that the main problems dealt with by the Commission drew any nearer consensual settlement. Perhaps some present themselves more starkly. One sequel of the War was that Poor Persons' Procedure—previously determined upon—became effective. The demand for it had been greatly strengthened by conditions due in some ways to the War. Between 1914 and 1919 a large proportion of our able-bodied men were on duty overseas, and great numbers of their women-folk had taken up unaccustomed tasks. Very many homes were broken up.

Whereas in 1914 there had been 1,348 petitions for divorce; in 1918 there were 2,689; in 1919, 5,763; in 1921, 3,464. The increase went on, and in 1934 there were 4,727 petitions. The statistics show the effect of Poor Persons' Procedure during the post-War years. In 1914, of the 1,348 petitions presented, Poor Persons' Procedure accounted for only 99. Of the

4,727 filed in 1934, practically three-fourths —3,726, in fact—were presented under Poor Persons' Procedure, and its effects were seen throughout the country. In London it accounted for 1,692 cases, and in the provinces for 1,584.

The contrast of a yearly average of eight or nine hundred decrees, one among about 8,400 families, during the years shortly before the War, and the figures of the years since the War, can only be properly understood if regard is had to some facts already pointed out. In 1921, 3,091 decrees, or one among about 2,500 families; in 1931, 3,764 decrees, or one among about 2,125 families; in 1933 and 1934 successively, 4,042 and 4,199, or one among about 2,000 families. What strikes the eye as regards 1921 and 1934 is what approaches a fourfold increase in the number of petitions for divorce. But in 1914 there were only 99 petitions under Poor Persons' Procedure. In 1934 there were 3,726, and the total number of petitions was 4,727.

Of the 4,199 decrees pronounced in 1934, 1,994 were obtained in suits conducted under Poor Persons' Procedure. Apart from this, 1,944 decrees were granted to ordinary litigants, and 1,944 decrees among a population of above forty millions gives an average of one decree among about 6,400 families. In 1911, as has been said, the current average worked out at one decree among about 8,400 families. The increased ratio is probably not wholly due to Poor Persons' Procedure. Take it that half the decrees granted in 1924 would have been got under old-time conditions: 2,100 decrees would mean one among about 3,900 families. If you bear in mind the events of the years since 1914, can you properly say that recent statistics show a prevalent popular disregard of the institution of marriage?

The statistics last cited are, as stated, statistics of divorce. Behind the proceedings out of which they arise there is a background illustrative of the possible difficulties of married life. There goes on day by day resort by aggrieved spouses to magisterial tribunals in respect of defaults other than those which warrant dissolution of marriage—among them cruelty, desertion, failure to maintain, and failure of parental duty. The report of a Home Office Committee issued in 1934[1] showed that magisterial orders in such cases had risen to as high a total as eleven thousand in a year, and it stated that some fifty thousand orders were said to be in operation. Whether complainants in such cases commonly have cause of action which would warrant a suit for divorce is matter of conjecture.

[1] Cmd. 4649.

The statistics do not deal with such subjects. This class of litigation has tremendous reactions on social well-being, and consciousness of this fact has drawn widespread attention to the proposition that an effective reconciliation is a far better thing for the man and woman concerned than the most drastic order justices can make.

Debates in Convocation and elsewhere, Bills in Parliament framed to facilitate amicable settlements of matrimonial differences, and a prolonged Inquiry before a Departmental Committee at the Home Office, have manifested the widespread anxiety there is for conciliatory action which should clear up grounds of complaint between man and wife before they lead to irreparable mischief. Such activities are not within the scope of this treatise, but a good deal of information respecting them can be found in the Reports of the Parliamentary Debates in the House of Lords, in November 1934, and January and February 1935, upon a Bill introduced by Lord Merrivale, which aimed at administrative action toward systematic resort to conciliatory procedure. The Bill received general support, was passed without Division, and is said now to be under the consideration of the Home Office Committee. One object of all such action is to obviate questions of divorce.

"WHAT SHOULD BE DONE?"

DESIGNS for replanning the domestic life of the community come from various quarters. What the qualifications or the personal record of most of the authors may be with regard to the things that matter may or may not be known. Such schemes do not command serious consideration. What has really to be determined is whether and to what extent changes such as those embodied in the Majority Report of the Royal Commission would be for the good of the community, and if so, what is the best means of carrying them out. Another thing, hardly less important, is some review of the law which would secure better than present-day conditions do, the well-being of some parties to marriage. There is a recent statute which has prevented headlong marriages of the very young. Resort to Scotland to get married is not frequent now, but it does happen. It could be put an end to by declaring such transactions void. Resort to foreign jurisdiction and pretence of acquiring domicil there in order to evade prohibition or restrictions existent here, has come to light at times, though not frequently.

More serious than the tricky proceedings just mentioned is a laxity with regard to marriage which arises from the non-existence of any proper provision for publicity, and a consequent lack of control where control might be exercised. The calling of banns may or may not inform the persons concerned in the matter. As to the posting of a notice in a Registrar's office—how many people are ever informed of it? Yet the published statistics show that such posting of notice is the preliminary of more than half the marriages celebrated in England and Wales. It follows that marriage can easily be brought about without any notice being given to persons in *loco parentis* of the parties. Under French law there are safeguards against the elemental risks to which these conditions conduce. Here, a Royal Commission in 1867, which had among its members lawyers of the highest eminence, recommended restrictions to guard against improvident marriage, and before the Royal Commission of 1909 many witnesses advocated the same change. Public notice is easily practicable, and direct notice to parents and guardians could be made a preliminary to lawful nuptials. The experience of other countries shows these things to be practicable. No reasonable critic could suppose they would encourage illicit sexual relations. On the contrary, they would tend to strengthen and dignify the marital relation, just to the extent that they demonstrate the will of the community to safeguard its vital interests.

If marriage were more strictly regulated, due control might well be substituted for the laxity about divorce which tends to increase among the class of people who have much regard for penalties but little for decency. As things are, divorce by arrangement is easily brought about by unscrupulous persons. An undefended divorce suit is a different thing from a suit planned without regard to the law by persons between whom there is no grievance. How to deal with the law-breakers is not an easy problem, but various methods have been discussed. Before the Royal Commission of 1909, Lord Mersey recommended that the guilty party in a divorce suit should be incapable of remarriage, but this suggestion has not seemed to command much support. A more effective deterrent would be to give to the competent Courts increased power to deal strictly with wrongdoers. An award of damages and costs may extend some satisfaction to an injured spouse: but it does not take account of public interests. No one supposes that persons guilty of fraud expiate their offences when they have been ordered to pay damages and costs. Why should a man who breaks up the home of another escape the proper consequences of criminous misconduct?

Safeguards could be brought into use. There are at present statutory enactments which, upon proof of specified offences, deprive a citizen of some rights of citizenship; for example, the electoral franchise, competence to fill certain public offices, right to receive beneficial grants. Perusal of the Elementary Education Act, 1870, schd. IV, I, Pt. I (4), the Forfeiture Act, 1870, c. 29, 2, and various Licensing Acts dating from 1870 onward, illustrate the proposition. Public interests are involved in the security of the home, and they could be proclaimed and vindicated by reasonable action in some such way as is here suggested.

Whether the grounds of divorce now defined by the relevant statutes ought to be extended has been much debated in recent years. It is a practical question, and cannot well be answered upon merely notional considerations. On the one hand you have the grievances of wronged spouses; on the other the interests of the community. Lord Gorell discussed the matter before the Royal Commission, and two passages from his statement may be cited to illustrate his opinion:

Some maintain that independently of religious considerations the interests concerned and objects to be attained are best secured by declaring marriage absolutely indissoluble.

On the other hand, it is strongly urged that those who hold these views do not sufficiently recognise the existing facts, those facts being that human beings are not ideal, that events occur which in fact end married life, that adulteries, desertions, cruelties, etc., take place, that dreadful misery is inflicted on innocent people and their children, and that a disregard of law takes place if release cannot be obtained, and that these matters do not occur in solitary instances, but to an extent which affects large numbers of people; and further that the necessity for intervention exists, and has always been recognised, even by ecclesiastical authorities who provide the inadequate remedy of separation in certain cases, and that the stability of society will be rendered firmer by mitigating the hardship of the law. In effect this contention is that the interests concerned and objects to be attained will be best secured by recognising the general permanency of the marriage bond, and, at the same time, recognising how in actual human life the object with which that bond is formed may be wholly frustrated with miserable and disastrous results.

No one who had the advantage of knowing Lord Gorell could fail to be touched by the poignant feeling conveyed in his reasoned presentment of "the alternative case." And, apart from personal knowledge, it must be felt that the vast experience and the anxious thought which moved him to speech upon such topics, enhance the value of what was said. Lord

Gorell, however, wished that a careful and settled judgment should be formed. No hasty action could promote the well-being of the community.

Definite as was the recommendation of the Royal Commission that the grounds of divorce available to suitors domiciled in England should be extended, no substantial advance toward extension has been made. Discussion goes on as of old. Responsible people in various quarters have urged—and from time to time do urge—that relaxation of the existing law cannot be indefinitely postponed. The Joint Committee of the Convocation of Canterbury and York lately expressed the view that "the question on what grounds a marriage may be dissolved must be faced in the light of existing circumstances." The extended grounds of divorce which are most commonly advocated and which were approved by the Commission, include these: Prolonged wilful desertion; cruelty involving danger to life or limb; habitual drunkenness of an aggravated kind; and sentence of death commuted to imprisonment for life. Overseas, within the Empire, modern legislation has dealt with most, if not all, of these proposals, so that experience of their effect is available, though not under conditions identical with those of our own people. Near at hand, malicious desertion which has continued for four years, entitles a complainant if the parties are of Scottish domicil, to a decree of dissolution of marriage.

VIEWS OF THE CHURCH

As a practical matter the question of granting by Act of Parliament extended grounds of divorce can well be approached in the light of the declared opinions of the Two Convocations in a recently published Report. Religious principles will surely affect the ultimate decision, and its grave seriousness cannot but be remembered at a time when there comes in view a possible parting of the ways whereby secular legislation may be enacted in such terms that the Church of England must inevitably be found dissentient. This possibility is plainly recognised in the Report.[1]

The Joint Committee say this:

> In the present conditions of general society it must, we believe, be conceded that, so far as secular legislation is concerned, some provision for dissolving the legal bond is inevitable. In a State wholly composed of persons who sought to live a Christian life, no provision of any such kind would be required. But once it is

[1] 1935; S.P.C.K., London.

allowed that England is not at present a nation wholly composed of such persons, and includes large numbers of people who definitely reject the obligations of the Christian religion, the question "on what grounds a marriage may be dissolved" must be faced in the light of existing circumstances. The grounds might, we are convinced, be severely limited, even in secular legislation. Further, we wish to register an emphatic protest against the way in which it is now possible to arrange a divorce, desired for quite different reasons, under the cover of an inferred act or series of acts of adultery.

As to the guiding motive in any action to be taken by the Church, the Report says:

The chief question for the Christian to consider is thus, viz.: "Taking into account the state of mind of a community in many respects non-Christian will the proposals in question make it easier for society as a whole ultimately to accept the Christian ideal?" Allowance must be made for the fact that rigid opposition by the Church may result in an increased unwillingness to listen to its message.

As to the Christian principle concerning marriage, the Report, as might be expected, speaks with absolute certainty:

The marriage of a husband and wife [it says] is "till death us do part"; it is a lifelong vocation or relation which not only ought not to be dissolved but also involves a moral and spiritual bond which cannot be finally terminated save by death.[1]

As to possible legislation which might make Divorce permissible on extended grounds, the Report says:[2]

> In the present condition of general society it must, we believe, be conceded that, as far as secular legislation is concerned, some provision for dissolving the legal bond is inevitable.

Dealing with the religious and social conditions which the anticipated changes would entail, the Report discusses the question of what should be the attitude of the Church toward persons divorced under a relaxed code.

> The Church [the Report says] must make it perfectly clear that . . . not only should there be no rights given for a second marriage to take place in Church in the lifetime of the former partner, but the Church should be free to make its own regulations for its own members, more particularly with regard to (1) the forbidding the use of the Church in the case of either party entering into another contract of marriage during the lifetime of the former spouse; and (2) the admission of such persons to the Sacraments and other privileges of the Church.

Responsible authority vested in the Bishop of the diocese concerned is recommended as

[1] Page 18. [2] Page 20.

the means of dealing with particular difficulties which may arise.

The Report deals also with what is sometimes called Civil Marriage.

> We should like [it says] to recommend an amendment of the law which now requires the whole Marriage Service to be read in cases where the parties to a marriage contracted at the Register Office desire to add . . . a religious ceremony carrying the blessing of the Church. . . . We think that another authorised form of Church service should be provided, allowing for the omission of those parts of the Marriage Service which are not appropriate for the religious ceremony after the civil contract. Such a privilege should not, however, be extended to any person who has been a party to a divorce suit.

That a period should be reached in the social development of England when the questions dealt with above necessarily command the attention of representatives of the Church must be matter of grave concern to those who realise the vital and all-essential importance of the marriage tie. That the Church should deal with them otherwise than in absolute candour is inconceivable. The Church cannot change the standard of its belief. The founder of the Faith Himself defined marriage for all who accept His words. Whether there shall be a Church Establishment—important as that has been thought—is a small matter compared with the testing question "Shall the Church be Christian?" If, as time goes on, the legislature should place marriage on some new footing, it may well be thought that, upon a vital issue, Church and State have arrived at the parting of the ways. Bearing in mind, though, that in the great majority of cases marriage is still solemnised as a religious ordinance, it seems unlikely that our people will suddenly take action to give effect to a different view.

How far the legislature can go without losing the concurrence of the great body of Christian people will no doubt be anxiously considered as time goes on. Civil marriage which has not the essentials of marriage as we know it, will not offer wholly attractive prospects to the persons most concerned. No English legislation can be visualised which would legalise concubinage or polygamy. Whether Parliament shall ever be empowered to sanction conditional marriage in the sense that there might be dissolution of the tie on the grounds of extension set forth in the Majority Report of the Royal Commission will be matter of keen conflict whenever such proposals are authoritatively made.

SOME POSSIBLE STEPS

Among the grounds of extension, a case involving least difficulty is probably that of prolonged wilful desertion; where that means, as it commonly does, the disappearance of one of the spouses. A familiar occurrence in proceedings relating to the administration of the estates of deceased persons is an application, after proper inquiries have been made, that the Court shall presume a missing person to be dead, and the presumption is made subject to limitations. In some of the worst cases of hardship arising from wilful desertion, the presumption cannot be made by the deserted spouse without the risk that upon reappearance of the absentee a second marriage must be regarded as bigamous, and is in the legal sense "null and void." There is herein an oppressive hardship. It would be avoided if in proper cases—not hastily or artificially but upon proper proof of relevant facts—the respondent in a suit founded on long desertion might be declared civilly dead, and the petitioner to be his lawful widow. An incidental effect would be to vest in her any assets to which upon his death intestate she would become entitled and to make any will of which probate could be obtained an effective testamentary disposition.

There is another juristic aspect of prolonged desertion on the part of a spouse. Assuming the absentee to be a normal person and to have lived with the deserted spouse on ordinary terms of conjugal affection, there is little room for doubt that sexual desires which were lawfully satisfied during marital cohabitation will be as potent when that has ceased. Proof of adulterous association with some third party may not be forthcoming. Yet it may well be that such association appears inevitable to those who knew the facts. At present, a presumption to this effect cannot be made, with due regard to the terms in which the relevant allegations in a suit for divorce have to be framed. A good many cases arise in which it would be perfectly reasonable. An amendment of the regulations governing the procedure could be framed which would invest the judge with authority to make the inference in any case where, upon the evidence, it should seem to him reasonable so to do. No laxity in the administration of the law would be encouraged by such a change. A competent judge would look at the matter the more strictly because of the generality of the question involved.

What is described as "cruelty" is one of extended grounds of divorce which have been commonly discussed. The first comment which experience supplies is probably that nothing in the law is more absolutely undefined than "cruelty." Words, looks, acts not involving personal violence; all of them may be evidence of "cruelty" in the sense in which that term is used in matrimonial causes. To set it up fictitiously, or to provoke it wilfully, is perfectly easy for unscrupulous people who have a sufficient motive. The notion that a spouse conjugally faithful will break out into acts of real cruelty is hard to conceive. Cruelty, too, has its appropriate penalties, and as between husband and wife they might possibly be made more severe than in other cases. If what is called cruelty is to be made a by-way for divorce, some remarkable developments may be looked for.

Habitual drunkenness, if it springs from evil living alone, is a vice against which the law makes some provision now. Normally it is not a solitary vice. It does not as a rule develop suddenly. If it has real relation to the marriage tie, it commonly has reactions there which give normal grounds for divorce. If it has not, can it be said otherwise to afford a sufficient ground for dissolving that tie? To make it easier to break the marriage bond than to dissolve a contract of civil employment would supply a strange commentary upon our ways of living.

The problem of the incurably insane is a most grievous one. If such an infirmity was latent at the time of marriage it might well be deemed a ground of nullity. If the condition has come about by reason of the stress of living, it is a calamity to all concerned. Does it call for pity, though, or for penalties? Who is to pronounce it "incurable," and if mental vigour returns, what is to be the plight of the victim? Little wonder that in past times those who have had to form definite opinions on this painful topic have more often than not concluded—with regret it may be—that when a man and woman take one another for husband and wife, it is, as the marriage service says, "for better, for poorer; in sickness and in health; till death do us part."

"Sentence of death, commuted to imprisonment for life." Death sentence for what offence? Then—the crime in question may be wholly foreign to the domestic life of the parties; treason or treason felony, perhaps. What if the unconvicted spouse was *particeps criminis*? What if the offence was of that class in which a wife, though participant, could not be convicted because she must be deemed to have acted under the influence of the husband? If the commuted death sentence is ground for divorce, what of a sentence of penal servitude for life? In such cases what interval is to elapse before divorce may be claimed? After what lapse of time is the title to sue for divorce to be deemed extinct? On what terms, if at all, is the competent tribunal to decide in what cases divorce shall be decreed? What tribunal is to be declared competent? All these questions cry out for sufficient answers. One may be that in cases where the facts warrant it the convict shall upon conviction be declared civilly dead.

LASTLY

When judgment comes to be given upon serious proposals for the amendment of the law of marriage, let us make sure that any change to be made shall be beyond question a beneficial change. Our English people have experience enough, and sense enough, to determine the matter. Past generations have supplied us with knowledge; the facts of everyday life supply the problems which that knowledge guided by honest minds, must solve. Let us bear in mind that marriage is an outstanding means of benefit, and that divorce is its enemy. So may we be guided in the right way.

For Product Safety Concerns and Information please contact our EU representative GPSR@taylorandfrancis.com
Taylor & Francis Verlag GmbH, Kaufingerstraße 24, 80331 München, Germany

www.ingramcontent.com/pod-product-compliance
Ingram Content Group UK Ltd.
Pitfield, Milton Keynes, MK11 3LW, UK
UKHW022158190926
475702UK00003B/93
* 9 7 8 1 0 4 1 3 5 3 1 7 1 *